PALAEOGRAPHY

AND THE PRACTICAL STUDY OF

COURT HAND

PALAEOGRAPHY
AND THE PRACTICAL STUDY OF
COURT HAND

BY

HILARY JENKINSON, F.S.A.

of the Public Record Office
F. W. Maitland Memorial Lecturer in the University of Cambridge

Cambridge:
at the University Press
1915

CAMBRIDGE
UNIVERSITY PRESS

University Printing House, Cambridge CB2 8BS, United Kingdom

Cambridge University Press is part of the University of Cambridge.

It furthers the University's mission by dissewwminating knowledge in the pursuit of education, learning and research at the highest international levels of excellence.

www.cambridge.org
Information on this title: www.cambridge.org/9781107427457

First published 1915
First paperback edition 2014

A catalogue record for this publication is available from the British Library

ISBN 978-1-107-42745-7 Paperback

PREFACE

THIS pamphlet is, with very little revision, a Paper read to Section IX of the International Congress of Historical Studies in April, 1913. I have not thought proper to alter it in any essential and that fact has, to some extent, conditioned its form; leading me, for instance, to confine my remarks upon *Diplomatique* to a paragraph and a footnote. It represents the ideas which have made me depart considerably from the usually adopted form of teaching preliminary to research upon medieval manuscript sources, during the three series of lectures and classes which I have given for the F. W. Maitland Memorial Trustees at Cambridge. But apart from this the importance of the series of documents which illustrate it made me anxious to print it.

I have been much indebted to my colleagues, Messrs C. G. Crump and Charles Johnson, while preparing it.

H. J.

May 1914.

CONTENTS

PAGE

INTRODUCTION

Palaeography as an essential preliminary to Research on Medieval History . . . ix

COURT HAND

The *Curia* . . . 1
The Courts of Chancery and Exchequer . . . 1
The purely Judicial Courts . . . 1
The Growth of Administration . . . 2
The three Varieties of Record Making:
(1) and (2) Copies and Registers . . . 2
(3) Miscellanea:
Records of non-Official Origin . . . 3
The Records of Private Administration . . . 4
The Close of the Medieval Period:
New Writing, new Administration, new forms of Documents . . . 4
The real Court Hand . . . 5
Summary . . . 5

THE SCIENTIFIC STUDY OF COURT HAND

Early Schools of Handwriting . . . 6
The Work of Administrative History . . . 7
What is Palaeography?
Palaeography and History . . . 8
Palaeography and the Reading of Documents . . . 8
Diplomatique . . . 10
Palaeography and the Dating of Documents . . . 10
Palaeography as an Exact Science:
The bulk of the Public Records . . . 11
The number of possible scribes . . . 12
The age of the scribe . . . 13
Environment . . . 14
Ignorance . . . 14
The habit of exact copying . . . 14

ILLUSTRATIONS

Plates I and II . . . *To face p.* 16
Plate III . . . ,, 18
Plate IV . . . ,, 20
Plate V . . . ,, 22
Plate VI . . . ,, 24
Plate VII . . . ,, 26
Plates VIII and IX . . . ,, 28
Plate X . . . ,, 30
Plate XI . . . ,, 32
Plates XII and XIII . . . ,, 34

CONCLUSION . . . 36

INTRODUCTION

Palaeography as an essential preliminary to Research on Medieval History

In this paper I wish not so much to communicate the result of research as to put forward a profession of faith. It is hardly necessary to dwell on the paramount importance to-day of Documentary Historical Sources: and the Science of Palaeography claims everywhere, claims unchallenged, a very prominent position as an essential preliminary to the study of the medieval sections of these. The Treasures which we in England possess in the way of Documentary, and in particular of Record, sources have, it has been declared on the best authority, no rivals in the world: on the other hand we are frequently told—we have been told so very recently by critics within our own gates—that our willingness and ability to apply ourselves to the necessary preliminaries, and among them particularly Palaeography, leave much to be desired. I would speak, if I may say so, upon this matter in three capacities; as an Archivist, not only loving Records for their own sake but also called upon as it happens to deal daily with large quantities of medieval documents of continually varying dates; as one who has in a small way attempted, at Cambridge, during the last three years to solve the question of giving in an economical fashion to ordinary historical students some slight incentive to and some general preparation for possible research work in the future upon English medieval sources; and as one who has assisted in the compilation of a comprehensive text book[1] upon the handwriting side of the same purpose. From these points of view I will venture to touch upon one or two features in that wealth of English sources to which I have alluded; and to examine the work of Palaeography in the light of them and their importance. If the examination is of the nature of criticism I hope it will appear that I wish not merely to pull down but also, and more anxiously, to set up.

[1] *Court Hand Illustrated*..., now in the Press. Many of the matters dealt with in the present paper are expansions of questions touched on in this Book.

COURT HAND

The various forms of writing in which English medieval documents (other than formal books) are preserved to us are all derived from an increasingly current writing of the same script which, remaining formal, gives us Book Hand; and are known to us collectively as Court Hand, that is the writing of the Courts. At the risk of saying what has been said before we must examine for a moment the meaning of this word and what it connotes, before we pass to our main subject.

The *Curia*

The original Court or *Curia* is the personal Court or *entourage* of the Monarch. The English *Curia* after the Conquest is highly administrative and in the processes of administration it assumes various aspects: beneath them is always the one *Curia*; but its appearance varies with the functions it is momentarily performing. There is for example the Chancery function: here one Officer is pre-eminent—the Chancellor presiding over his scribes; other members of the Court act merely as witnesses to those instruments under the King's Great Seal which it is his duty to prepare and issue. Then we have the Court sitting as a board of finance, presiding over the Annual Audit; in this case the Treasurer takes the lead, but other Members nearly all assist—Constable, Marshal, Chamberlain, Justiciar all have their seats at the Board.

The Courts of Chancery and Exchequer

Both in the Chancery and in the Exchequer business increases both in bulk and in scope; and with this goes the natural accompaniment, an increase in the number of subordinates and in the number of deputies: the Chancery and Exchequer have more and more to do and grow more and more professional in character. It is in a third aspect of the Court, however, that professionalism shews itself earliest and most strongly—the judicial aspect. Very early indeed the legal activities of the King, his Justiciar and the members of his Court—the sessions *Coram Rege*—have to be supplemented by itinerant judges: soon even this is not enough; the centralising and solidifying genius of the early Norman Kings works so fruitfully that a second, permanent,

The purely Judicial Courts

Court must be created in London—a Court with whose operations the King and his own *Curia*, travellers over the Realm, can have little to do: we have definitely established the Justices of Common Pleas, a definitely professional administrative class.

Administration[1] is founded on precedent, that is on memory; and it grows with the adoption for its own uses of artificial memory, that is of writing. What we claim for England, what is perhaps stronger in this than in any other country, is the early, continual, universal, crystallisation—formalisation—of administrative processes in the minutest, the most remote departments of life: and, accompanying this, first a necessary accumulation of pieces of artificial memory, of writing, relating to each of these minute departments of life; and then an unnecessary but most fortunate conservation of these in quite extraordinary quantities long after the probability of their use as precedents has disappeared.

The Growth of Administration

But it is not enough to say, as we may say from the foregoing, that the course of English medieval administration has left us an enormous collection of documents: the development of formalised administration carried with it, and the peculiarities of English history and English character have preserved to us, a wonderful collection of what we may call in the strictest sense Records: that is to say, that the writer of the Courts had not only to deal with originals, which issue and seldom return to be preserved in the Official Collections; that is a comparatively small part of his business: there are also the two immensely important and bulky varieties of Copies of originals which issued and Registers of proceedings which took place[2]. No country can shew such examples of them as can England, with its score of great continuous series running down from the 13th century almost to the present day[3], all of them officially produced, preserved throughout in official custody and for official reference. I suggest that the importance of these *full, regular, authentic, officially preserved Records*

The three Varieties of Record Making:

(1) and (2) Copies and Registers

[1] By Administration I understand the regulisation of any side (social, industrial, legal, military, ecclesiastical) of the affairs of a person or community of persons by constituted authority.

[2] The word *Record* applies properly and originally only to process at law. I use it here, as it is generally used, to mean a document which forms part of the collections in the Public Record Office: and in order to cover all the contents of that building we must define a Record as a document forming part of an official administrative process and preserved, for the purposes of official reference, in official custody. In a large number of cases, including the two classes here under consideration, we may add that the documents are officially written.

[3] They begin in the Exchequer, the *Curia Regis* (Judicial) and the Chancery in the reigns of Henry II, Richard I and John respectively.

is one to which a greatly increased comparative attention is due. The Enrolment or Register is too often treated as a place where lost originals may by good fortune be retrieved: I should rather say that such Records have in England an importance beside which that of originals is almost insignificant. Their immediate importance in their present connection, however, is the early, continuous, and highly varied currency of handwriting which goes with them and is largely fostered and developed by the peculiar circumstances under which they were produced[1].

We have mentioned two varieties of Record making; but there is a third besides those which I have labelled Copies and Registers —the great class of regularly filed Originals, the Ancient Miscellanea which at one time were preserved by every Court. I would dwell for a moment on the Record character of these. This does not depend on the officiality of their writing; for although many of them may have been official originals returned (such as writs), probably quite half of them cannot claim that character, being merely supplementary details for more important Records or casual Memoranda or even documents of private origin and meaning which have been drawn into the Public Collections by such an accident as (*e.g.*) the escheat of a property, with its muniments, to the Crown: it depends rather upon their being filed, at some time, in an official connection with other official documents and preserved for purposes of official reference.

(3) Miscellanea;

Records of non-Official Origin

Two further points may perhaps be mentioned in connection with these. First there is the fact that they exemplify, obviously, the earliest kind of Record keeping; series in the other two classes have been formed by the separation off and subsequent standardisation of bulky classes of Memoranda or Copies from these Miscellaneous Collections; cases are not wanting where the border line between the formal Enrolment or Register on the one hand and the file of Miscellanea on the other is very slightly defined; and the process of differentiation is always going on[2].

[1] To take only one instance, handwriting will very obviously be affected in the case of a scribe whose chief or sole duty is to copy a large number of documents, in the purpose and original writing of which he had probably no share, on to a long roll as quickly as possible.

[2] A good instance of this is supplied by a comparison of the medieval common law jurisdiction of the Court of Common Pleas and that of the Chancery; and of their respective Records. The Records of the Court of Common Pleas are, of course, bulky rolls of uniform membranes: those of the Chancery's Common Law jurisdiction are in phraseology like them; but since this jurisdiction never attained to great importance they themselves never attained to a more dignified form than that of most un-uniform membranes of Memoranda scattered over the Chancery's Miscellaneous files.

The second point is this. The handwriting of these originals among the Miscellanea is chiefly important for our present purpose because it is so largely non-official: but it must be remembered that in England the influence of the official model was on every side of administrative activity remarkably strong; great interest attaches to the unanimity and closeness with which even the instruments of private or semi-public administration—Court Rolls, for instance, the Registers of Corporate Bodies, original private deeds, or, if I may select an instance I have myself to a slight extent worked out, private tallies of receipt—conform themselves to their contemporary parallels in public life; this conformancy is seen in fashions of all kind, in shape, in phraseology and—equally—in writing.

The Records of Private Administration

It will be seen that two circumstances—on the one hand the habit of the Official Record maker of preserving among his Miscellaneous Memoranda all kinds of documents which were not official in origin but which by some official accident came into his hands and had for him an official interest, and on the other the imitative habits of the Record makers of lesser, private, administrations—these two circumstances have joined with other more normal influences to preserve for us in the Collections made by the King's Courts a remarkably catholic body of pieces of medieval writing. So much, for the moment, for the medieval Courts and the general characteristics of their Records.

The Close of the Medieval Period:

It is when we arrive at the period of letter writing that Court Hand loses its character of omnipresence. Simultaneously, or very nearly so, with what is usually considered the end of the medieval period in England—the reign of Henry VII—we find reforms, sometimes revolutionary, instituted in various Courts; in the Exchequer of Receipt, for instance, new Officials come to the front and with them new Records: almost at the same time appears a new class of Administration and Administrator, an institution which English Archive practice distinguishes from the old *Courts*—the *Department*, the Office of the Secretary of State; whose Records are *State Papers*, with, very soon, a special home of their own in the State Paper Office. The very word *Paper* indicates a change of fashions and it is about this same time that we have imported into England the new Italic handwriting, which gradually—very gradually—ousted the decadent current forms of Court Hand and which was the ancestor of our modern script.

new Writing, new Administration, new forms of Documents

The Court Hand thus displaced was a very slovenly and decadent form indeed; but by this time the Courts had established in their more formal Records a limit of currency beyond which their handwritings did not go. The writing thus established, or modifications of it, they continued to employ long after the Italic hand had become almost universal in ordinary usage: they even developed among themselves distinct contemporary varieties of it, and from this practice of theirs comes the use of the words *Court Hand*. The name, however, has been applied retrospectively to cover all those classes of documents the existence of which previous to 1485 I have adumbrated.

The real Court Hand

Summarising, therefore, we may say that when we speak of *Court Hand* we are referring—if the medieval period is our mark—in the first place to all kinds of that current writing whose first step in its development out of Book Hand may be seen in the volumes of Domesday. Further, we are referring (1) to the documentary remains, formal and informal, of the Courts of Exchequer, Chancery, Common Pleas and King's Bench, (2) to the documentary remains of all kinds of private and semi-private Administrations—the Administrations of the Palatinate, the Borough, the Guild, the Manor, or any agglomeration of property or rights which leads to the collection of deeds, letters and memoranda, of *titres*, of evidences of its privileges and its proceedings. Touching the first class of these we have suggested so far that its most formal manuscript remains—its Registers and Copies—are of immense bulk and of an importance very much undervalued for the subject we have in hand: touching the second, the Records of private or semi-private Administration, we may say that accidents of various kinds have resulted in numerous specimens of the Records produced by the various activities which it includes being preserved among the Public Records—mainly among the Miscellanea of our first class. The Public Records in fact, the Archives in the Chancery Lane Repository, include the bulk of some of the most important classes of medieval documents and representatives of practically all: and to the writings in which all these classes of documents are cast the general term *Court Hand* is applied. It is a loose but convenient name.

Summary

THE SCIENTIFIC STUDY OF COURT HAND

It is not to be supposed, of course, that there were not distinguishable styles of handwriting in the various Courts for some time before the words Court Hand could be correctly used in the sense I have described. From about the time of John the most formal Exchequer hand—that of the Pipe Roll, and, later, the Enrolled Accounts which split off from it—large, angular and carefully written, is generally distinguishable from all others employed in the English Courts: the most formal hand of original Grants, *i.e.* of Charters and Letters Patent, which most nearly resembles this Pipe Roll hand, is yet again distinct: while the Enrolment hands of the Chancery and the Registering hands of the Plea Rolls and the Exchequer Memoranda Rolls after going through phases of general currency settled down during the 15th century into conventional forms which differentiate them from other hands and even from each other: and apart from these there is a general residuum of highly current writings varying almost infinitely according to circumstances. It is however to a rather earlier period than this—roughly the 13th and the early 14th centuries—that I wish chiefly to direct attention; and during this period the distinction between the current hands of most Enrolments and Registers and that of Miscellaneous Deeds and Memoranda of all kinds is not marked.

Early Schools of Handwriting

Knowledge of the circumstances and persons responsible for a given series of Records may enable us at various times to detect the spreading of influences from one of the classes mentioned above into another, to place and account for certain familiarities and unfamiliarities, habits of thought, fashions of abbreviation, and so forth. Thus the knowledge that Stapleton was at the Exchequer or that the Tellers were, at a given time, supplanting the Deputy Chamberlains might well throw light upon the script peculiarities of a Receipt Roll: the discovery that at a certain period most of the items in the Pipe Roll were written up beforehand, gives us a criterion of the speed at which that Record was written: the information that Plea Roll and Inquisition *post mortem* particulars and even Original Letters Patent were often supplied, ready written out, by the parties concerned must have a strongly modifying influence upon our opinions concerning their handwritings and concerning the relations of State clerks and public scriveners: the fact that the Justice's clerk at one time made up those lists of fines which we meet in the Exchequer may serve a similar purpose. Taking a slightly different standpoint we might suggest that by compiling a list of the clerks in any given Office we could establish something in the nature of a succession with a possible inheritance of characteristic tricks of handwriting in the series of documents which that office is known to have produced; that private deeds, or even such official documents as assessments for taxation, being written locally by the parish priest might be found to fall into divisions according to the different houses of Religious in whose gift various livings lay; or that the detailed history of scriveners' guilds, if it could be worked out, might enable us in another way to establish the existence of undoubted schools of handwriting in divers places.

The Work of Administrative History

But where in all this does the science of Palaeography come in? I have endeavoured to indicate above a few possibilities of what would be undoubtedly discoveries of palaeographical interest. I would submit, however, that in all these the starting point is supplied by history, generally by the history of that Administration which is directly responsible for the making of the Records. The story of the succession of scribes of the Exchequer is written in the Rolls which detail the payment of their wages; the particulars of Henry VII's reforms at the Receipt come to us through the papers of a law suit between the Clerk of the Pells and the *Scriptor Talliarum*; the intrusion of the family solicitor into public documents is a matter of occasional points of internal evidence; the activities of the Justice's clerk may be traced to an Exchequer order: everywhere the tale is the same—the History of Administration supplies the initial explanations of Palaeography.

What is Palaeography?

Now Palaeography may be defined as a science which examines the forms of individual letters in every obtainable stage of their evolution from the earliest known form down to that of the present day, classifying them according to the origin and succession of their forms, the writing materials used, the way in which the pen or other instrument is held, and so forth. It follows, of course, that the student trained in Palaeography should first be able, though this is really an incidental matter, to say without question what any given form of letter represents—to detect for instance in what looks at a certain part of the medieval period like a capital *M* what is really a capital *S*; and secondly should make some pretensions to the assigning of any given form to a certain class, a certain date, and even a certain locality. From these two powers of the palaeographical student it is usually argued firstly that every one who is to deal with ancient handwritings should be trained to read them by a course of Palaeography and secondly that a man so trained will be able to assist the historical student by assigning a date to his documents. It is by these arguments that Palaeography, as a practical aid to the practical student of History, must stand or fall.

So far as concerns documents not in Book Hand the science of Palaeography (medievally speaking) was invented (as indeed was also *Diplomatique*) to deal with documents of an early date, when writing was comparatively little applied to administration; a date from which, consequently, survivals are very few and those, from the point of view of the information they offer to the critic of their structure and date, not fully developed. But, once again, it must be considered in the present paper in a strictly practical light, the light of the claim which it makes, or which is made for it, to be of essential utility to historical research upon English medieval sources as a whole—a whole of which the early documents above described form a part so insignificant as to be almost negligible. What we have to ask ourselves is: how far is the overloaded student of History to be saddled with special preliminary studies before he is allowed to undertake research work? or, supposing that we grant the necessity of such preliminary studies, are we quite sure that Palaeography is an essential one of them?

Palaeography and History:

Palaeography and the Reading of Documents:

Now for the purposes of mere reading, Palaeography cannot be considered necessary. Scores of students have indisputably learned to read adequately, even well, without ever troubling to memorise a palaeographical rule, without even knowing why a particular sign is called Tironian or how the earliest contractions were concerned with the name of God: in all the great workers of the past in England there is to be found no trace of palaeographical training. I would not, of course, deny for a moment that minute knowledge of the way in which a given letter was habitually formed (say for instance, the medieval *g*, with its three essential parts of upper bow, lower bow and final horizontal stroke) may upon occasion lead to a definite conclusion in reading when all other aids fail; nor that the palaeographer can, for example, tell the student reader that *t̃n* means *tamen* and not *tantum*. But the vast majority of the difficulties which beset the reader of medieval English documents—such difficulties as the resolution of a large number of minims into *i*'s, *m*'s, *n*'s and *u*'s, the distinction between *O* and *E*, or the question of the meaning of a marginal *ex̃* or *p.e.*[1]—cannot be cleared up by the palaeographer; and on the other hand it is extraordinary how few are the cases where more than one sense is possible in a given passage. To know what must be there, what the document must mean, is, in fact, a much greater assistance than to know what, palaeographically, the letters appear to represent; and to the necessities of the context Palaeography is no guide.

It is necessary to observe that the purpose of this paper is not to decry the value of Palaeography as an independent study, far less its interest; nor to deny its necessity in any historical field save that of English Court Hand and English official documents with their adjuncts. I would emphasise, however, once again the essentially administrative character of all English Court Hand documents: in the comparatively rare cases—I wish that I had space to point out how singularly rare they are—where even private documents[2] have no connection with Public Administration and where, consequently, the explanation of difficult points in them cannot be sought among Public Records, they have generally an administrative connection, equally sufficient for explanatory purposes, with others in the same collection as themselves.

It is not my business here to point further the conclusion which should have emerged inevitably from the foregoing remarks that not *Diplomatique*[3]

[1] One might add—an even more obvious instance—that Palaeography is powerless to aid in extending any of those suspensions (so common in later Court Hands) which represent an inflexion.

[2] Taking only the case of a private deed touching the transfer of land we may point out that if—as very frequently occurs—it is in the form of a fine or recovery there will be a mass of documents relating to the transaction preserved by the Court of Common Pleas; alternatively, if it takes another form, it will very often be enrolled, for safety, upon the dorse of the Close Roll; it may often, again, be subsequently confirmed, in which case it will be transcribed on the Patent or Charter Roll; if it relates to land held in chief a licence to alienate will be a necessary preliminary (Patent Roll and probably an Inquisition *ad quod damnum*) and later it may be cited or even quoted in Inquisitions *post mortem*: there are further numerous possibilities of the property being involved in a law suit and the deed quoted on a Plea Roll or of the Exchequer becoming interested and preserving a copy of the document among its Memoranda: while if the land in question ever falls into the hands of the Crown the actual deed will come into the Public Records with the other muniments of title.

[3] *Diplomatique* is the Science which studies all matters touching the form of documents and, particularly, their phraseology: it tells us, for instance, that Henry II referred to himself as *ego* and *me* in his Charters while Richard I said *nos*. Three things follow: (1) as its name implies it is interested in originals more than in copies; (2) if two documents are duplicates in form it takes no account of the fact that their position in administration makes their significance completely

but the history of Administration—Public Administration in all its branches and its most minute details, and Palatinate, Ecclesiastical, Borough, Manorial and all other kinds of Private and semi-Private Administration—is the one thing necessary for the explanation of our English documents; nor to give instances (there are many) where lack of this, not of *Diplomatique*, has led the most distinguished users of Public Records into false conclusions. But I may justly mention the fact that it does so emerge because, if I am right in the statements I have made with regard to it and if in addition the actual deciphering of that writing which we call Court Hand can be well and practically learned by, in effect, mere practice, then it may be true (the justification of this paper is that the writer believes it to be most urgently true) that we require in England a much larger number of students to work upon Records for the express purposes of Administrative History—that unwritten science; but it is not true that we want them preliminarily trained in *Diplomatique* in the sense in which that highly organised science is usually understood; and, though a previous study of facsimiles may save them much time, it is equally untrue that we want them trained in scientific Palaeography.

Diplomatique:

But we have still another point to deal with; for if Palaeography is not necessary in order to teach us to read it may yet be necessary in order that we may learn to date our documents: this is the second and, after an absolute essentiality, the highest merit which Palaeography can claim in the position of an adjunct to History. Let us examine then the further proposition that Palaeography as an exact science ceases, or becomes overwhelmingly difficult, where English Records, as series of importance, begin. I should like to adduce a few of the more obvious considerations which contribute to this view.

Palaeography and the Dating of Documents

Palaeography as an Exact Science:

Apart from the fact that during the whole of the finished, active Record keeping period, which begins about 1200, a large majority of Records date themselves, the first and most important consideration I have to suggest is that of bulk. I will take at hazard the eleventh year of Edward II—a date when governmental activity, as reflected in Records, had not reached

distinct: it will use indifferently a Chancery Inquisition or the Exchequer duplicate, though one is the return to a writ and the other the voucher to an account; (3) it treats documents *per se*; the fact that a particular letter under the Privy Seal is the warrant for a letter under the Great Seal does not particularly concern it, unless that fact induces a change of phraseology.

anything approaching its most prolific state—and examine the documentary remains of its Administration[1]. I need hardly remind the reader that we are deliberately excluding here all Private Records, except such as now figure among the Public Records; and even those we can only mention.

the bulk of the Public Records:

I should preface this statement by remarking that a Chancery Roll may be taken as consisting of any number up to 25 or 30 large membranes. The Exchequer Rolls are, relatively, very small at this period and perhaps the same modest estimate may be applied to them; but their membranes—except in the case of the Receipt and Issue Rolls—are twice the size of the Chancery ones. The same may be said of the lesser Plea Rolls; but the Rolls of the great permanent Courts are getting near to the period of their full size, when their membranes may run into hundreds.

The Chancery, then, supplies us in this regnal year with a Charter Roll; two Rolls of Letters Patent; a Fine Roll; part each of Extract, Gascon, Roman, Scottish, and Treaty Rolls; a Close Roll; parts of two supplementary Close Rolls; and a Roll of Writs for Issue (*Liberate*): turning to the Warrants for the issue of these "Great Seals" (not always a complete series by any means) we find four files, each containing perhaps a hundred writs; among those Returns by Inquisition, with writs attached, which often formed a preliminary to the issue of Chancery letters we find three large files of Inquisitions *post mortem*, eight files of Inquisitions *ad quod damnum*, and three of Miscellaneous Inquisitions: there is besides a considerable residuum of Miscellanea of various kinds.

The Exchequer yields much material. In the Receipt department we have six Rolls of Receipt and Issue and a little *Jornalia* Roll (giving daily and weekly balances); the original Tallies of receipt have perished but there is a fragmentary series of original Writs of *Liberate*. In the Exchequer of Audit we have, of course, the well known and bulky Pipe Roll (a single roll of this would make a very large volume if printed) and its copy the Chancellor's Roll, while accounts other than those of the Sheriffs' (*i.e.* the enrolled accounts of the Keeper of the Wardrobe, the Escheators, and so forth) are represented in the membranes of the Foreign Accounts: when we come to the remains of those preliminary accounts and vouchers of all kinds which preceded audit we find, of course, a very large number of documents, each numbering as a rule anything up to ten membranes; thus the Wardrobe produces eleven such accounts; the Sheriffs' Administrative

[1] I am indebted to my wife for the compilation of these statistics

Accounts two; the Customs five; the Fines, Amercements and Estreats, relating to the proceeds of justice, one complete account and parts of nine others; and altogether we have over 60 of these accounts to deal with—this in a year when the most numerous kind (that relating to Subsidies) is entirely wanting: the current business of the Exchequer is reflected in two Memoranda Rolls and one *Originalia* Roll (extracts from its own Rolls sent over by the Chancery): and finally the Exchequer, like the Chancery, has also a residuum of Miscellanea to shew us.

There was a Parliament in this year and its activities are marked by a Roll: but the Writs and Returns of Members have survived for only two counties: here again we have also some (Parliament and Council) Miscellanea in both the Chancery and the Exchequer[1].

Turning to the side of Justice, we find that this year gives us four King's Bench Plea Rolls, five Common Pleas Plea Rolls and one Exchequer Plea Roll; a Marshalsea Roll; two Rolls of the Courts of Wales and Chester; and the whole or parts of 19 Rolls kept by Justices on commission: further we have the Feet of Fines (copies of the most common form of deed for the transference of land) to the extent of 44 whole or part files. There are no Judicial Miscellanea for this year and the Writs have perished.

To these have to be added a very considerable number of Private Records belonging to this year now in the Public Record Office—Ministers' Accounts, Court Rolls and original deeds; and the much larger number of documents of the same description in other Public and in Private Collections[2]. And we must conclude by emphasising the fact that, while many years before this date we should find a quantity of Records almost equally large, not many years later the number would be many times larger.

the number of possible scribes:

A second consideration induced by this first one is that of the very large number of scribes whose work has come down to us though, in a large majority of cases, we are ignorant of their personalities; not to mention the great number of those who do not even live for us by this anonymous survival of their work. To begin with there is the crowd of official scribes: the Chancery scribes, including not only those who wrote original letters patent, charters and so forth, but also the scribes of documents under the lesser seals, the scribes of the

[1] The medieval Records of Parliament are distributed between the two Courts.

[2] To realise the size to which the medieval collections of a Private or a semi-Public Administrative body may go one has only to give the slightest glance at one of the fuller Reports of the Historical Manuscripts Commission.

enrolments, the scribes who wrote the already vast number of original writs which issued in judicial proceedings: there are the Exchequer scribes in four important and busy departments: there are the Judicial scribes who have left us in the Plea Rolls testimony of their own and the Justices' activities and who besides had the writing of all the very numerous judicial writs (or writs of process) which issued out of their various Courts, not to mention the numerous memoranda of panels of jurors and so forth which, like the process writs, have generally perished. Then there are all the scribes who had to compile for the Chancery or Exchequer the reports or accounts of such Royal Officers as the Escheators[1]. Besides all these there is the vast class of local writers who wrote the private letters and deeds or the private Manor Rolls not a tithe of which has come down to us; or again the local collectors and writers (to mention only one class of documents) of accounts and assessments for Subsidies. It can be no exaggeration to say that so early as the beginning of the reign of Henry III there was scarcely a place of the smallest importance in England which had not a scribe of some sort living in it; and we may add that there is not one of these scribes whose handwriting may not have been in large or small quantities preserved to us among the Public Records or elsewhere.

Surely in the face of such facts it is idle to pretend that any science can either cover with minute exactitude so wide a range of documents or on the other hand supply us with any common factors necessarily applicable to writers so many in number, distributed over so wide a space of country, in an age when means of communication were definitely bad, and practically all of them unknown to us in the matter of their age, origin, habits and standing.

Other difficulties:

There are, however, many lesser, yet still considerable, difficulties in the way of the palaeographer with which I have not yet dealt. With regard to the question of age, for instance, it has to be remembered that of any two clerks writing at one time similar, or parts of the same, documents one might be 60 years of age, the other 20; and this in a period when handwriting was undergoing constant and definite change: instances are not unknown where two contiguous pages in a Register are written in styles so distinct as to belong in appearance to dates a generation apart. Environment or early

the age of the scribe:

[1] There are many indications that the Sheriffs and Escheators must have maintained local offices which not only dealt with a considerable volume of business but also supported a considerable permanent staff.

upbringing suggests, again, obvious possibilities of the most remarkable peculiarities of writing. And we cannot leave out the probability of personal idiosyncracies of all kinds—any constant user of Records may collect hundreds of instances in a very short time.

environment:

Of more importance is the question of yet another unknown factor—the comparative ignorance or knowledge of a scribe. It is a safe maxim in Record work that ignorance on the part of a scribe must never be presumed, but the opposite of that statement is equally true: thus I give at the end of this Paper (Plates I and II) two instances of remarkably skilful work in the way of forgery by scribes of whom one at least appears to have been singularly ignorant of documentary matters other than actual writing: on the side of pure ignorance may be quoted the scribe who breaks off suddenly in his copy of an original, which is still preserved to us and is quite legible to the modern scholar, with the despairing remark *plus non legi potest*: and most of the mistakes made by modern beginners in reading—such for instance as the mistaken reading of the 14th century *W* as *lb*, or the 15th century *x* as *p*—seem to have been made at some time by a medieval scribe.

ignorance:

Curious instances of this kind might be multiplied, as might the collection of other facts relating to the medieval scribe tending all to the same purpose. The mention of copying, however, leads me to a remark upon one more factor of some importance. Copying at length was common in all classes of English medieval documents. Bishops' Registers, for instance, are often full not only of letters sufficiently drawn out but also of replies quoting the first letter in full and even of further replies quoting both the preceding; the formidable habit of the English Kings of quoting in their charters the full text of older deeds or charters which they confirmed is another manifestation of the same spirit; which, again, gives us wills quoted in full in Inquisitions *post mortem*, Royal Writs often most unnecessarily copied at full length in the notes of legal proceedings, and so forth. In fact the habit appears in every kind of document; and there are traces of very curious effects springing from it. Thus the scribe, unable to read, may endeavour to copy exactly, with disastrous results (particularly in the case of Saxon Charters); or, coming to a letter, a capital for instance, which is not so familiar as to be formed without thought in the established contemporary manner, he may unconsciously imitate the form he has before him in a deed perhaps fifty years old; or again he may (undoubted instances occur) deliberately archaise: from any

the habit of exact copying

one of these may result such a palaeographical anomaly as the *M*, or beaver-tailed, form of capital *S* in a Richard II Charter Roll, or the open-topped superior *a* reappearing in the 15th century.

But I must not linger over the fascinating subject of medieval scribal peculiarities. The instances I could offer must naturally be slight but very numerous ones—the cumulative evidence of continually occurring indications. For the same reason I could not hope to offer a sufficient number of examples for complete ocular demonstration. I have ventured however to put together a dozen illustrations, partly because they present almost unknown (most of them, indeed, recently discovered) documents of considerable interest; partly because they at least illustrate in a small way some of the points of difficulty which, I have suggested, make exact palaeographical work an impossibility from the 13th century onwards.

It should be noted that while Plates I and II are somewhat reduced the remainder shew the exact size of the originals.

ILLUSTRATIONS

Plates I and II represent the two forged charters mentioned above. They are examples, particularly skilful from a palaeographical point of view, of what was a fairly common practice in the 14th century, fostered, one may suppose, by either carelessness or corruptibility in the enrolment scribes of the Chancery,—the forging of charters which were to be presented for royal confirmation; but where they are most remarkable is in the fact that the forger has fashioned not an alleged previous confirmation of earlier grants but the actual original grants of the 12th century. The two are, if I may use the expression, different shots at the same object. Curiously enough the first is the one which was duly confirmed by Edward III though it is, apart from its writing, a clumsy affair, the address and witnessing clause betraying it hopelessly. It blunders besides over the name of a witness whom it calls Roger Bishop of York. This forgery has unfortunately been facsimiled as a genuine Henry II charter in the first part of the *Facsimiles of National Manuscripts.* The second charter, though it was not apparently used, is a finer piece of work—indeed, but for the fact that it again comes to grief over the same witness whom it calls Roger Bishop of Evreux (he should actually be Rotrou Bishop of Evreux) it might well escape detection.

Two points with regard to these plates may be specially noted: (1) that a skilful scribe of the time (probably) of Edward III was capable of falling into such notorious errors as the confusing of York and Evreux; (2) that the handwriting of the time of Henry II—a period in which anyone would be inclined to allow the science of Palaeography full scope—may be imitated so well as to deceive (as I think the second at least of these examples would deceive) even the most skilled palaeographer.

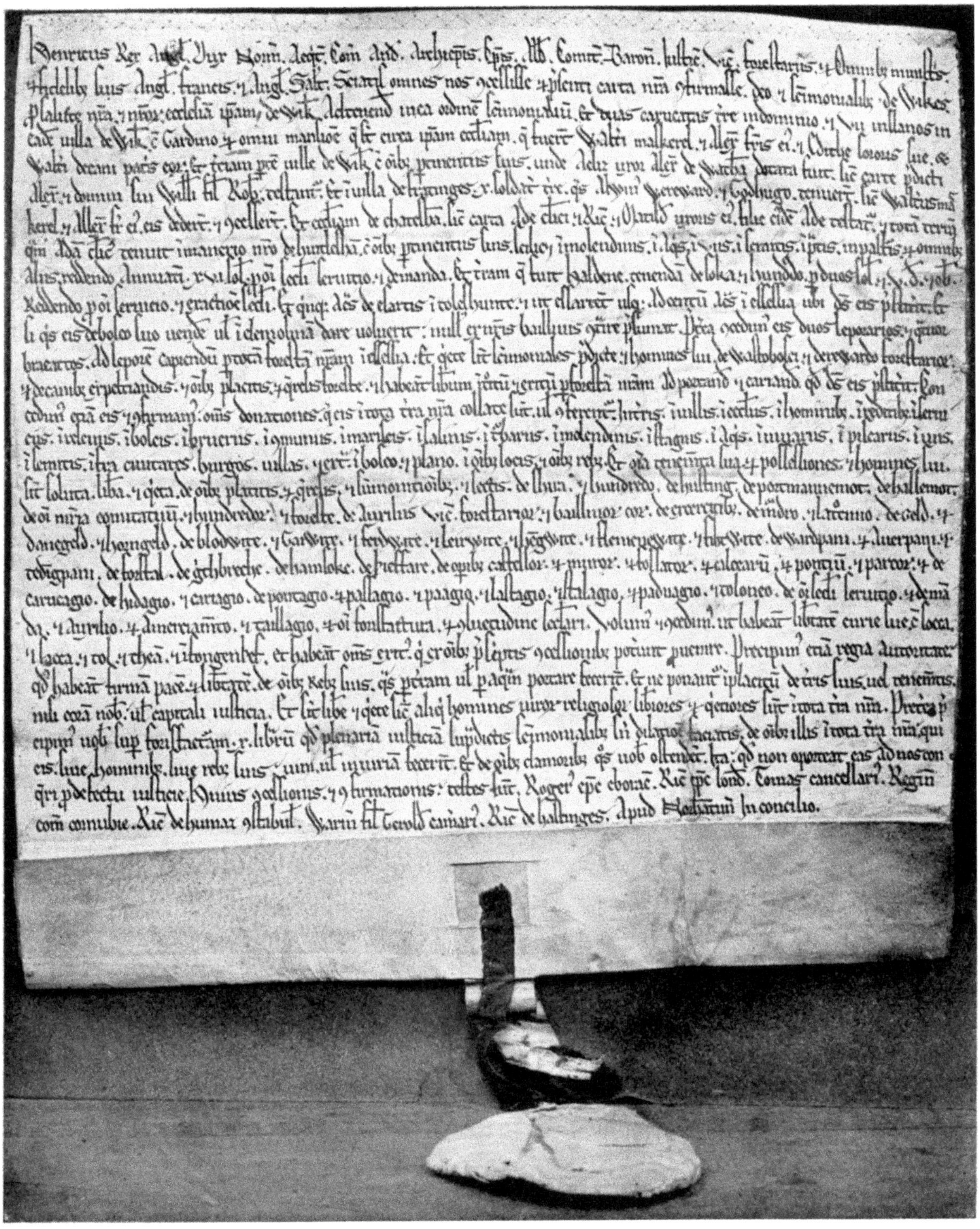

The remaining Plates display documents all of the same kind—they are all assessments for a tax of a fifteenth. They illustrate well some of the matters dwelt upon above—the wide local distribution of quite competent scribes in comparatively early times; the possible effects of age upon a scribe; the tendencies to archaism, intentional or unintentional; the influences of training or environment. The form of words employed is fairly constant being as a rule no more than the name of a person followed by a list of his possessions with the valuation of each attached; at intervals we may expect a *Summa* of the preceding paragraph together with a *Summa* of the fifteenth leviable. I will venture to give a slight detailed description of each of these specimens of handwriting before proceeding to draw a few general conclusions.

PLATE III

This is an early type of writing strongly suggestive of the Pipe Roll hands of the latter part of Henry II's reign; from which every letter in it could probably be paralleled. Noteworthy points are the distinct formation of every letter, the Book hand abbreviation for *pre* in *precium*, the open-topped superior *a*, and the absence of floreation in the tall strokes. The *Q* of *Quindecime* in the fifth line, the almost Roman *S* in *Summa*, the carefully formed *x*'s with the top right hand limb bending outwards are three out of a number of interesting points touching individual letters.

This and Plate VI will be found reproduced in *Court Hand Illustrated*.

Plate III

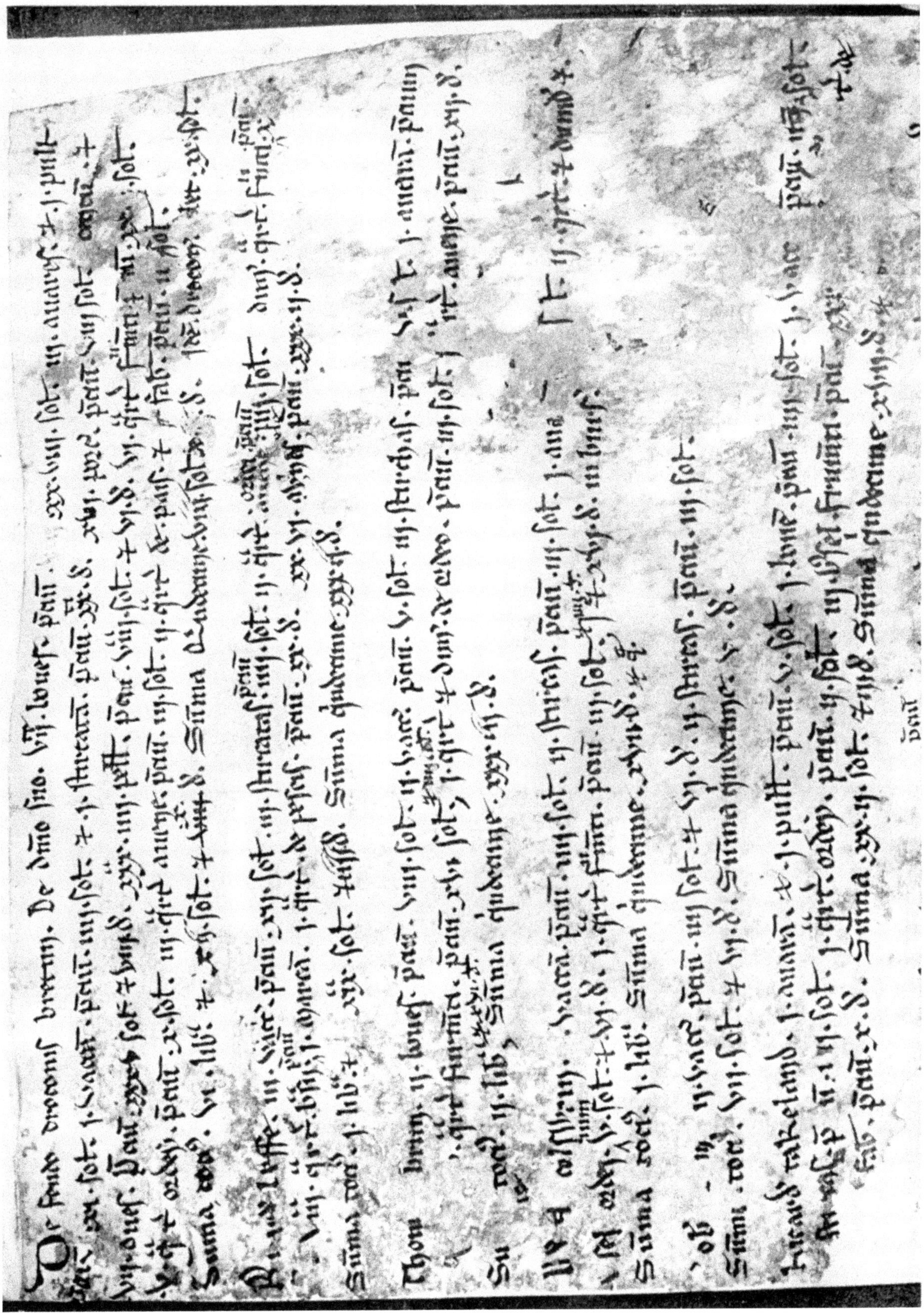

PLATE IV

This is of a similar character to the last but slightly less formal. There is a distinct tendency to run together consecutive letters consisting only of straight minims; notice for instance the *iu* of *precium* in several places and *iuuencam* in line 6. In other points the hand is still of quite an early type: the capitals *D* (*l.* 1), *N* (*Nicolaus* in *l.* 8) and *R* (*Rogerus* in *l.* 18) are obvious instances of this; as are the *k* in *Askebi* (*l.* 1) and several other small letters.

Plate IV

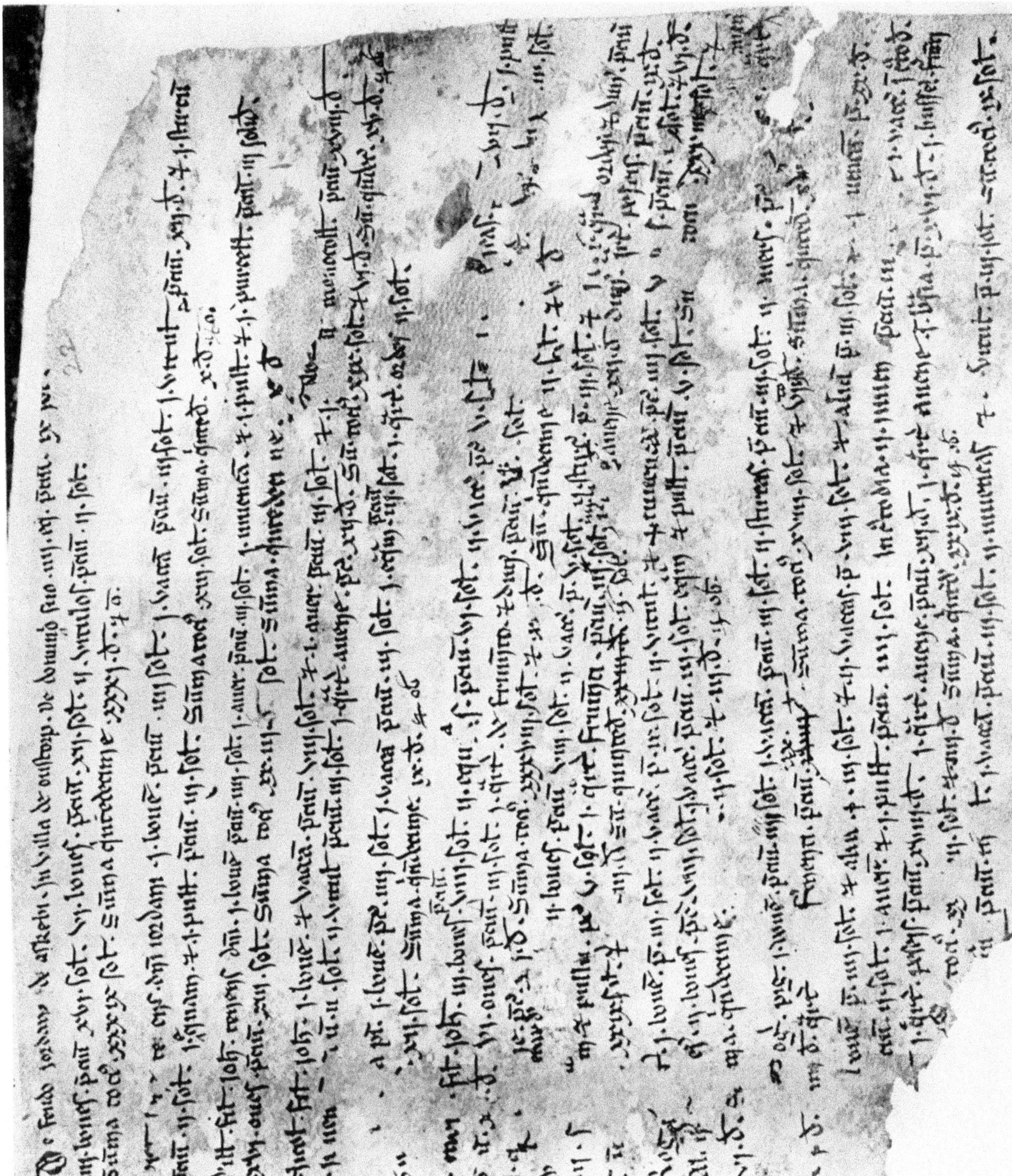

PLATE V

Is chiefly interesting as being clearly the work of an aged or infirm scribe. He does not use the Book hand abbreviation for *pre* but on the other hand he has frequently the ÷ abbreviation for *est*—a special sign which disappeared early. On the whole one might incline to describe it, on account of the obvious weakness of the scribe, as being of a rather later date than its general appearance would suggest. From the point of view merely of the form of the letter the curious *W* of *Willelmus* in the third entry is of interest.

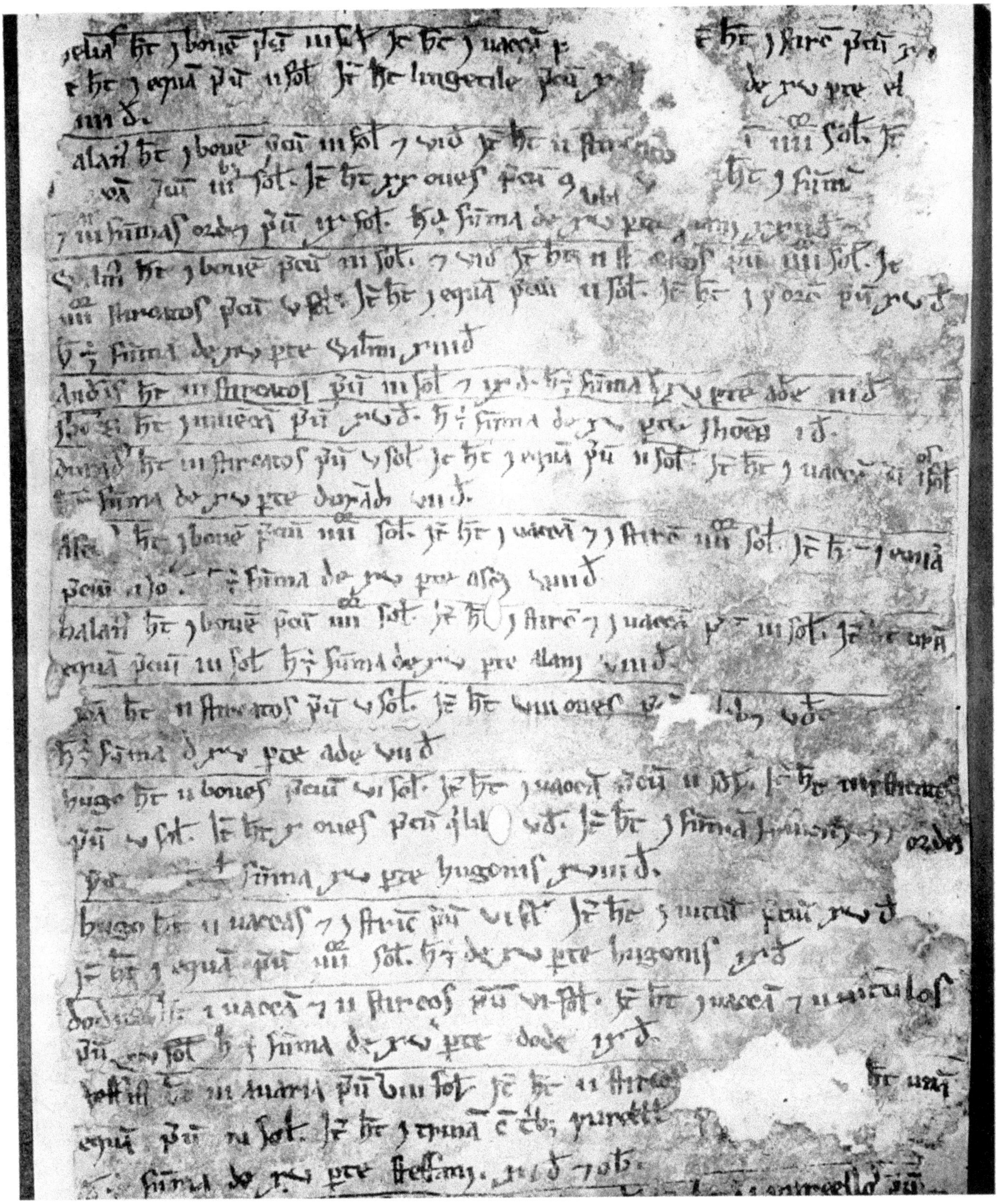

PLATE VI

Here we have a distinctly less formal hand, suggestive to some extent of the second, or simpler[1], Charter hand of the Henry II period. The capitals may be noticed particularly in this connection: *T* with its otiose vertical stroke; the curved *J* of *Johannes* and *Jurati*; the *R* with its exaggerated foot in *Radulfus*; the *H* of *Heidur* (all the foregoing are in the second line); the rather dashing *F* opening the second paragraph; the *R* in *l.* 15—even more typical, with its narrow head, than the first example mentioned: similar evidence is that of the beaked and floreated tall strokes seen (*e.g.*) in the *h* of *habet* (*l.* 11). The half-capital uncial *M* of *Modulum* (*l.* 13) is worth noticing; superior *a* has the closed top; in several places *x* has a freer character than in the preceding plates (for instance in *l.* 7); long *s* with its turned over head is almost everywhere worth noticing; and there are a large number of other indications of interest.

[1] Good examples of this are to be found in Delisle's *Atlas*, Plates V (no. 7 bis), VII (107A), VIII (31) and XXVI (497); and in a very charming charter in the Public Record Office (Duchy of Lancaster, Royal Charters, 26) belonging to (about) the year 1164 (*Court Hand Illustrated*, Plate VII, A).

Plate VI

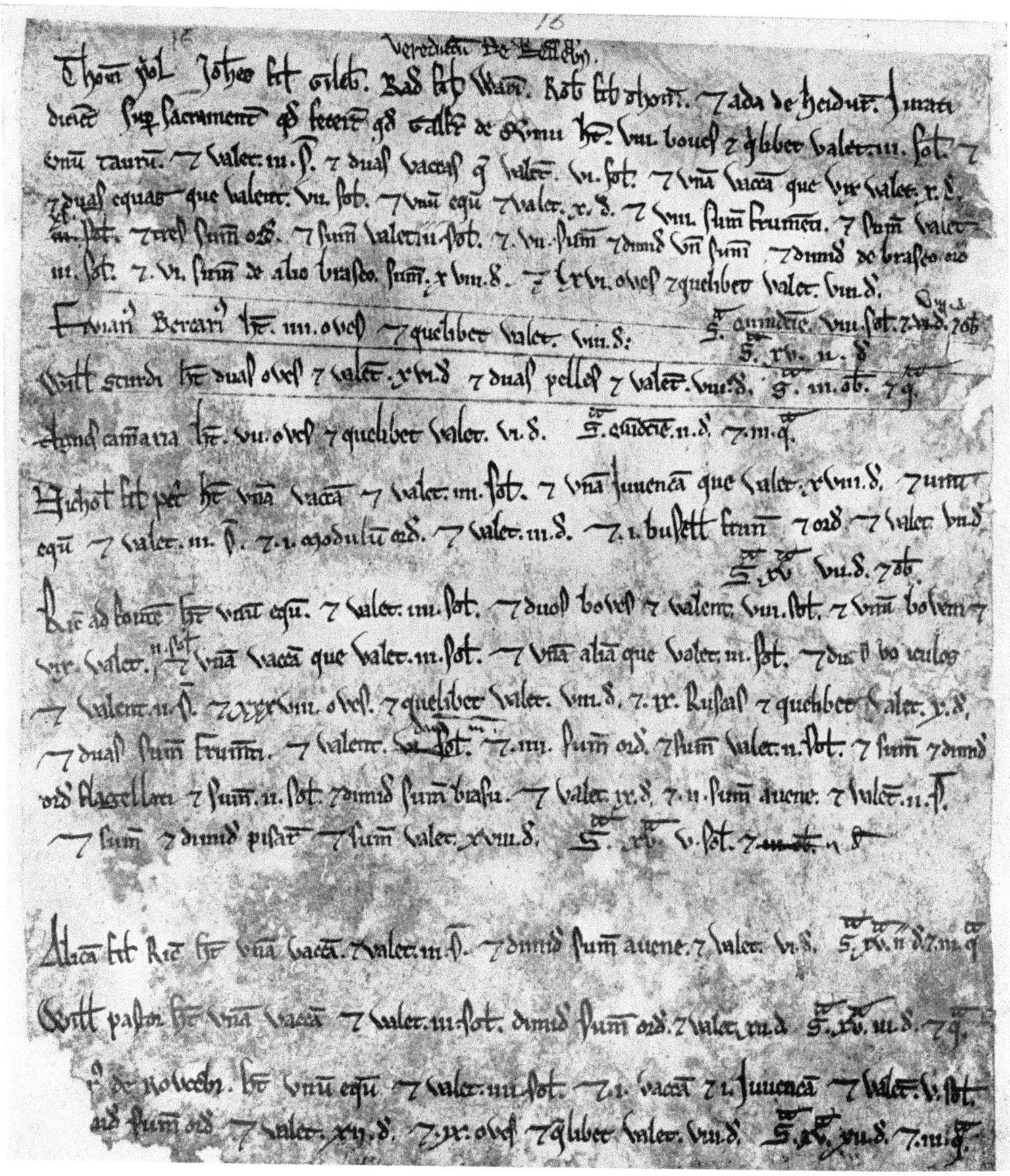

Veredictum de Bellebi.

Thom' p'p' Johes fil' Gileb'. Rad' fil' Wari'. Rob' fil' Thom'. 7 Ada de Heidun'. Jurati
dicunt sup' sacramentum quod fecerunt quod Galfr' de Grimi h't. viii. boues 7 quilibet valet. iii. sol. 7
unu' tauru'. 7 valet. iii. s'. 7 duas vaccas q' valent. vi. sol. 7 una vacca que vix valet. x. d.
7 duas equas que valent. vii. sol. 7 unu' equ' 7 valet. x. d. 7 viii. sum' frumenti. 7 sum' valet
iii. sol. 7 tres sum' ord'. 7 sum' valet ii. sol. 7. vii. sum' 7 dimid' vii sum' 7 dimid' de braseo ord'
iii. sol. 7. vi. sum' de alio braseo. sum' xviii. d. 7 lxvi. oves 7 quelibet valet. viii. d.

Ema' Bercari' h't. iiii. oves 7 quelibet valet. viii. d: S'. omnium. viii. sol. 7 vii. d. 7 ob
S'. xv. ii. d.

Will' scurdi h't duas oves 7 valet. xvii. d 7 duas pelles 7 valet. viii. d. S'. iii. ob. 7 q.

Agnes camaria h't. vii. oves 7 quelibet valet. vi. d. S'. omnium. ii. d. 7. iii. q.

Nichol fil' pet' h't una vacca 7 valet. iiii. sol. 7 una iuuenca que valet. xviii. d. 7 unum
equ' 7 valet. iii. s'. 7. i. modiu' ord'. 7 valet. iii. d. 7. i. busell frum' 7 ord' 7 valet. viii. d.
S'. xv. viii. d. 7 ob.

Ric' ad Tune h't unu' equ'. 7 valet. iiii. sol. 7 duos boves 7 valent. viii. sol. 7 unu' bovem 7
vix valet. ii. sol. 7 una vacca que valet. iii. sol. 7 una alia que valet. iii. sol. 7 duos boviculos
7 valent. ii. s'. 7 xxxviii. oves. 7 quelibet valet. viii. d. 7. ix. Ruscas 7 quelibet valet. v. d.
7 duas sum' frum'. 7 valent. ~~[illegible]~~ sol. 7. iii. sum' ord'. 7 sum' valet. ii. sol. 7 sum' 7 dimid'
ord' flagellati 7 sum'. ii. sol. 7 dimid' sum' brasii. 7 valet. xx. d. 7. ii. sum' auene. 7 valet. ii. s'.
7 sum' 7 dimid' pisarum 7 sum' valet. xviii. d. S'. xv. v. sol. 7 ~~[illegible]~~ ii d.

Alicia fil' Ric' h't una vacca. 7 valet. iii. s'. 7 dimid' sum' auene. 7 valet. vi. d. S'. xv. ii d. 7. iii. q.

Will' pastor h't una vacca 7 valet. iii. sol. dimid' sum' ord'. 7 valet. iii. d S'. xv. iii. d. 7 q.

[illegible] de Roucebi. h't unu' equ' 7 valet. iii. sol. 7. i. vacca 7 i. iuuenca 7 valet. v. sol.
[illegible] sum' ord' 7 valet. xii. d. 7. ix. oves 7 quelibet valet. viii. d. S'. xv. xii. d. 7. iii. q.

PLATE VII

This is a very interesting hand, exemplifying, but much more strongly, the characteristics noted in the previous one. Its resemblance to the simpler form of Charter hand of the reign of Henry II goes really beyond that type of writing; in fact almost any letter or word in it might be attributed, if it were isolated, to those Enrolment hands (to be seen in the early Patent, Close and Charter Rolls) which were themselves developed out of this simpler Charter writing; though the Enrolments would shew a good many currencies of writing and other characteristics (*e.g.* the floreated tall stroke) pushed considerably further than they are in our present example. From another point of view, it might be compared with certain rare deeds still preserved where an all but equal degree of currency and a similar smallness of writing are found at a rather earlier date: an instance of this is a beautiful little private deed now in the Public Record Office belonging to the year 1177[1].

It is to be noticed that in the matter of *i*'s, *m*'s, *n*'s, and *u*'s this document is fully current: the long *s* with its currently made head is also of interest. Most typical, however, is the general appearance of the script with its backward slope; its dash to the left of strokes below the line and to the right of those above; and its general air of free and rapid, yet regular, writing.

[1] Ancient Deeds, L.S., 49. The text of this deed is printed in the Pipe Roll Society's volume of Charters and a facsimile in *Court Hand Illustrated* (Plate VII. C).

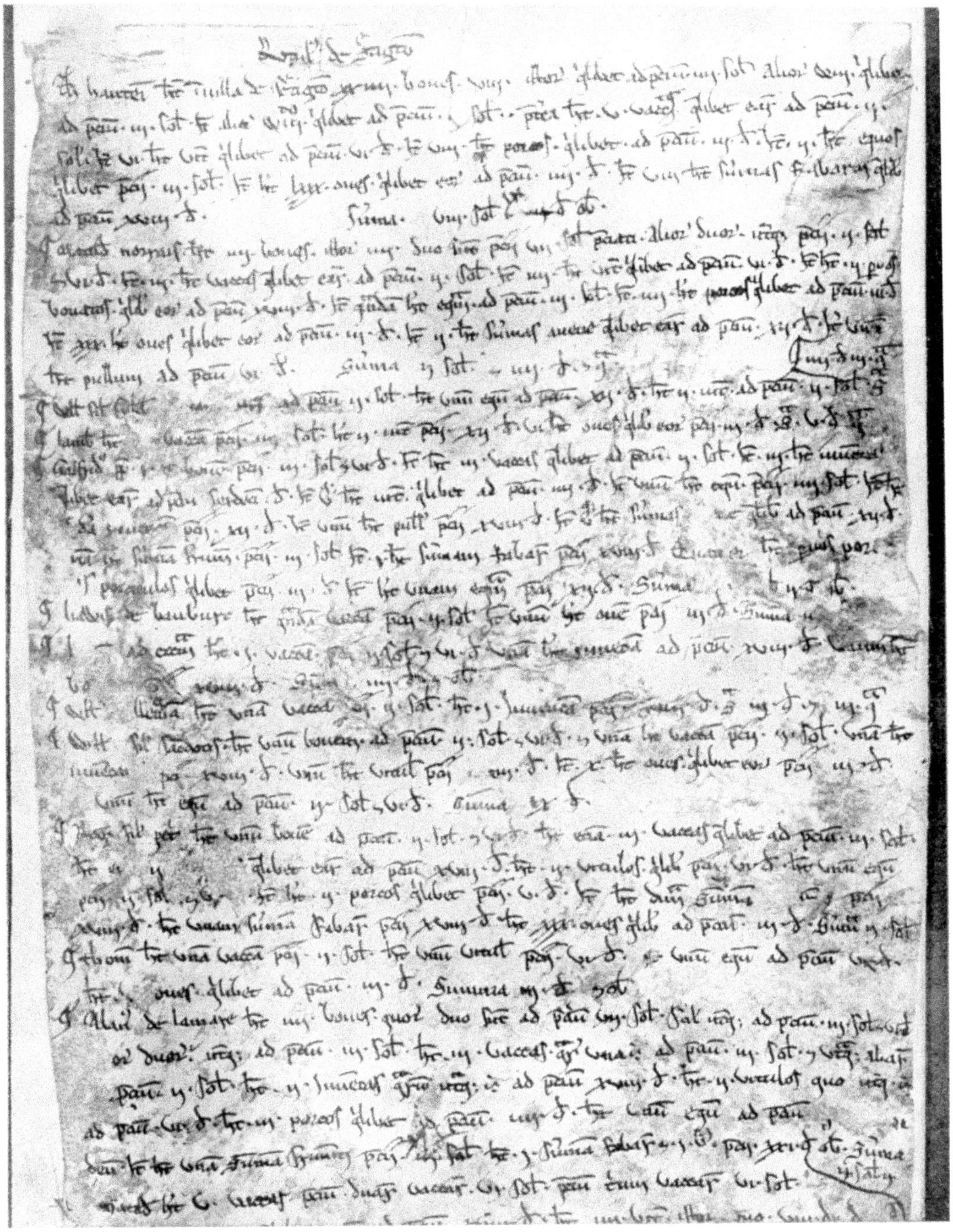

PLATES VIII AND IX

Plate VIII does not shew such a pretty hand as that of the preceding. It is of a higher degree of currency, bearing about it more evidences of the effects of Enrolment writing; but the narrower and more angular letters it gives us belong rather to the style of the early informal Enrolments of the Exchequer—the Receipt Rolls of the reigns of John or (very early) Henry III. Among many instances of the advance seen in this writing are the *E* of *Estimacio* in *l.* 1 of the second column (which may be contrasted with the *N* of *Numerus* in the same line) and the *G* of *Girardi* six lines lower; with the elaborate *R* of *Ricardi* near the foot of the other column, the turn over of the top of *v* throughout, and other indications. On the other hand the current writing of *m*'s, *n*'s, and other letters is not so marked.

Plate IX is a similar hand though not so closely like that of Plate VIII in general appearance. The *E* of *Elsi* (*l.* 13) and several examples of *S* with a heavy exaggerated tail are to be observed; also the current making of *a*, *A*, *d*, and other letters: and the use of contrasting thick and thin strokes, more noticeable here than in Plate VIII, is of importance.

Plate VIII

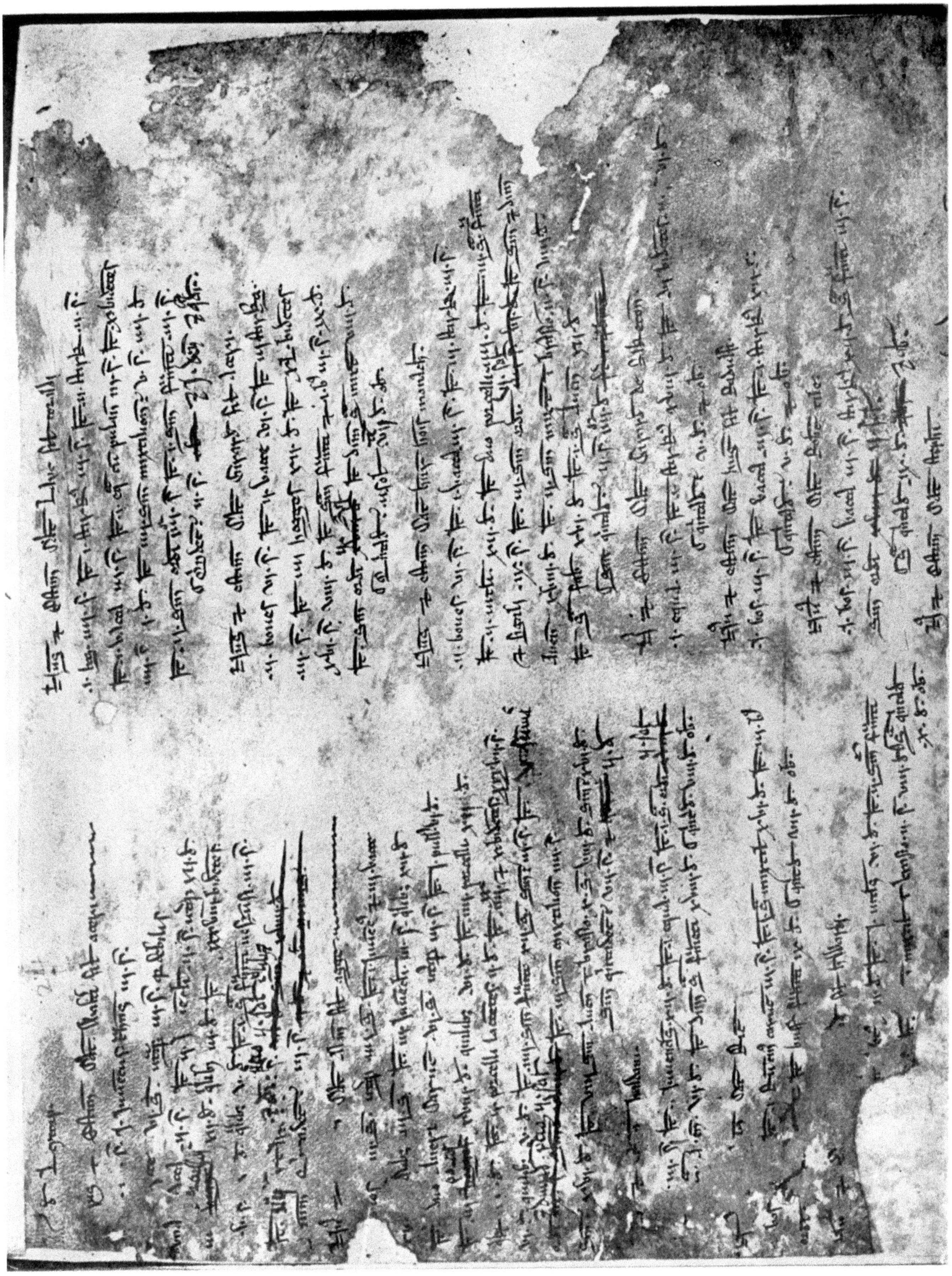

Plate IX

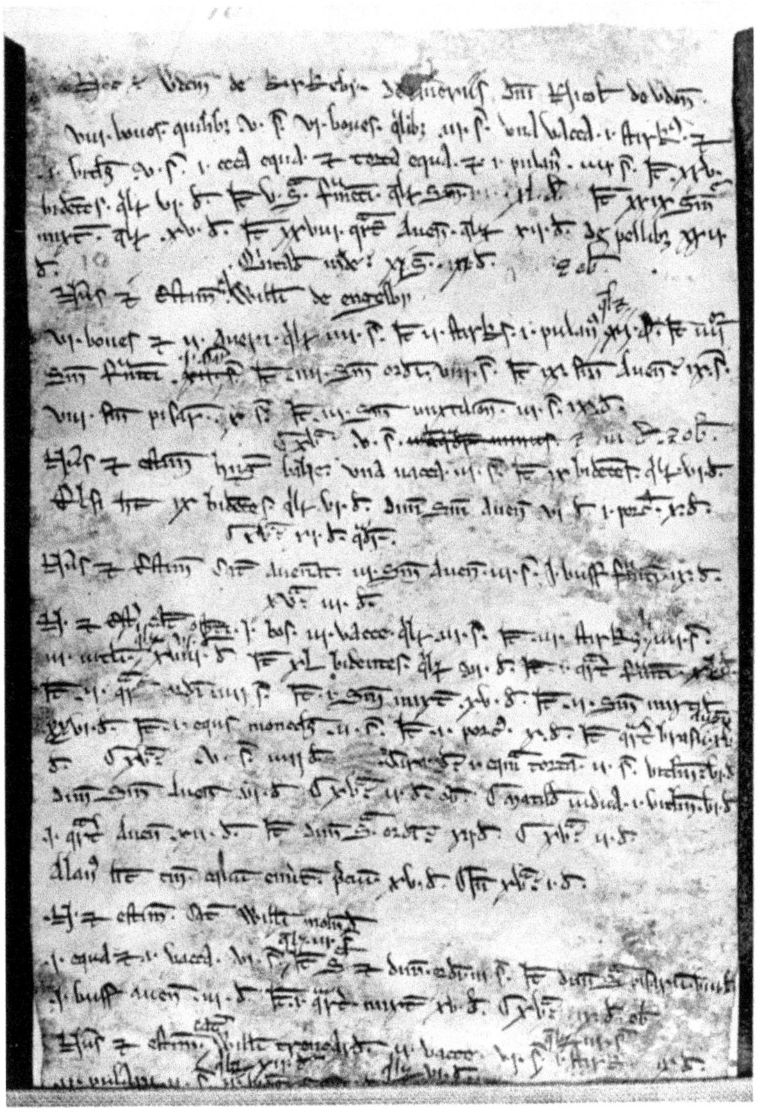

PLATE X

With this plate we get back to the tendencies of the Chancery Enrolments; or even to those of the earliest Plea Rolls, for the writing is very hasty as well as being highly current. It might also be compared with a number of private letters, of about the period of the reign of John, which will be found among the class of 'Ancient Correspondence' in the Public Record Office. The line beginning *Alexander de Lafford' Clericus* near the bottom of the document is a good example of this scribe's methods; the *L* of *Lafford'* with its floreated head and square base and the following examples of *ff*, *d*, and *c*, are all of interest. The same may be said of the undistinguished *m*'s, *n*'s and *u*'s, *x* with the head of its second arm turned inwards, and other indications of quick writing which appear throughout.

Plate X

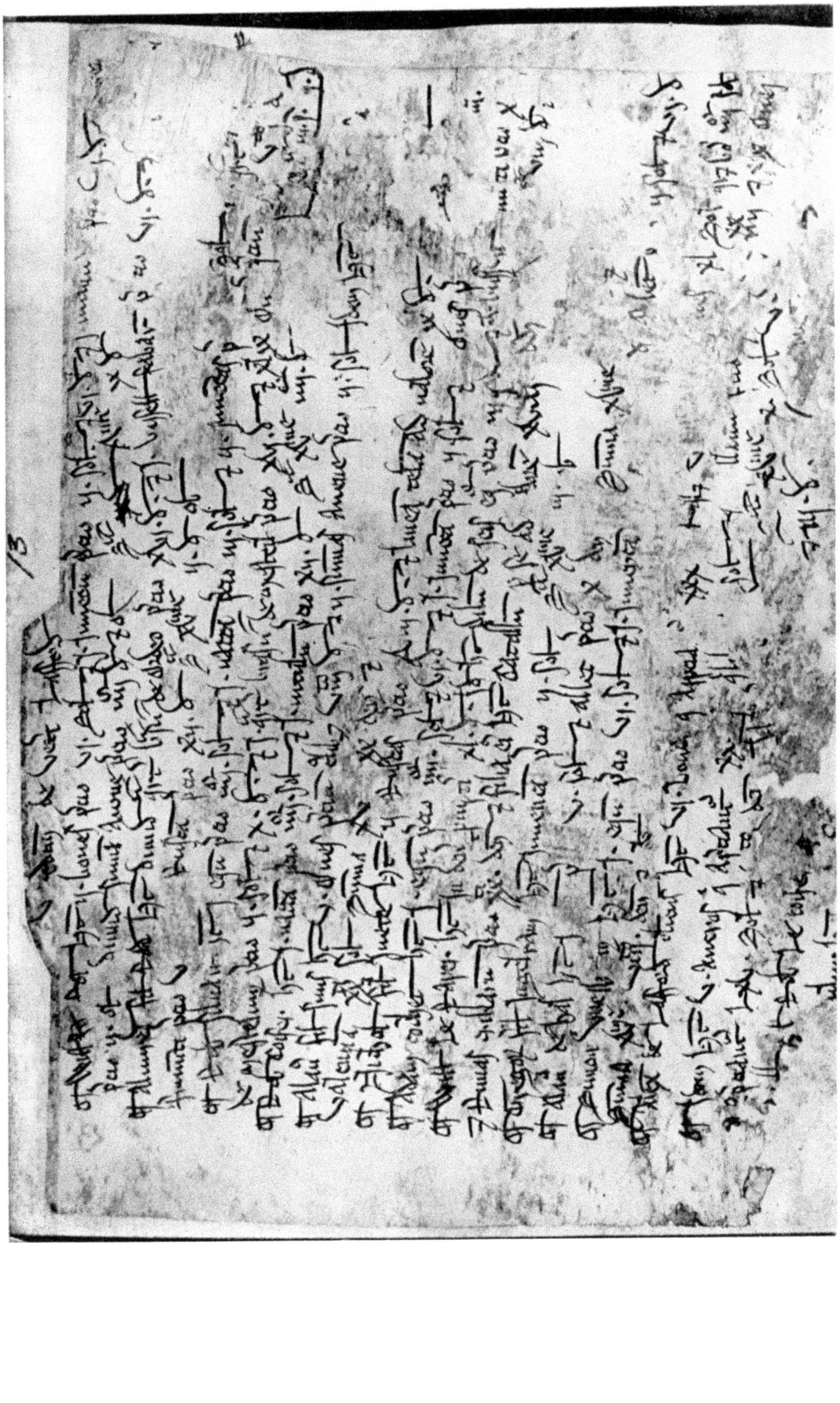

PLATE XI

In this plate we go at once to a quite advanced Enrolment hand. All possible letters are made currently and connected with ties which are naturally made (not, as is usually the case in the earlier current hands, deliberately thought out and so to speak added on to the scribe's conception of one or other of the letters they connect). But besides this all the other well-known characteristics of the Chancery Enrolment hand, at the period when it had become fully current but had not yet lost the taste for ornament, are to be seen here. The capitals—the *H* with two or three unnecessary horizontal bars, the *G* with its final horizontal stroke prolonged and turned upwards, the *D* with an additional vertical stroke, all shew this. So do many of the small letters—the *d* made all in one action, with its angular upper bow; the completely horizontal final stroke of *k*; the *v* with its first stroke prolonged upwards and bowed; the *x* with its second stroke produced below the line and recurved. Finally we have not only the highly floreated tall strokes of *J*, *h*, *l* and *b*, but also the right hand limb of this floreation bent into a complete loop which acts as a tie with previous letters.

Needless to say the above are only the leading ones among a large number of prominent features.

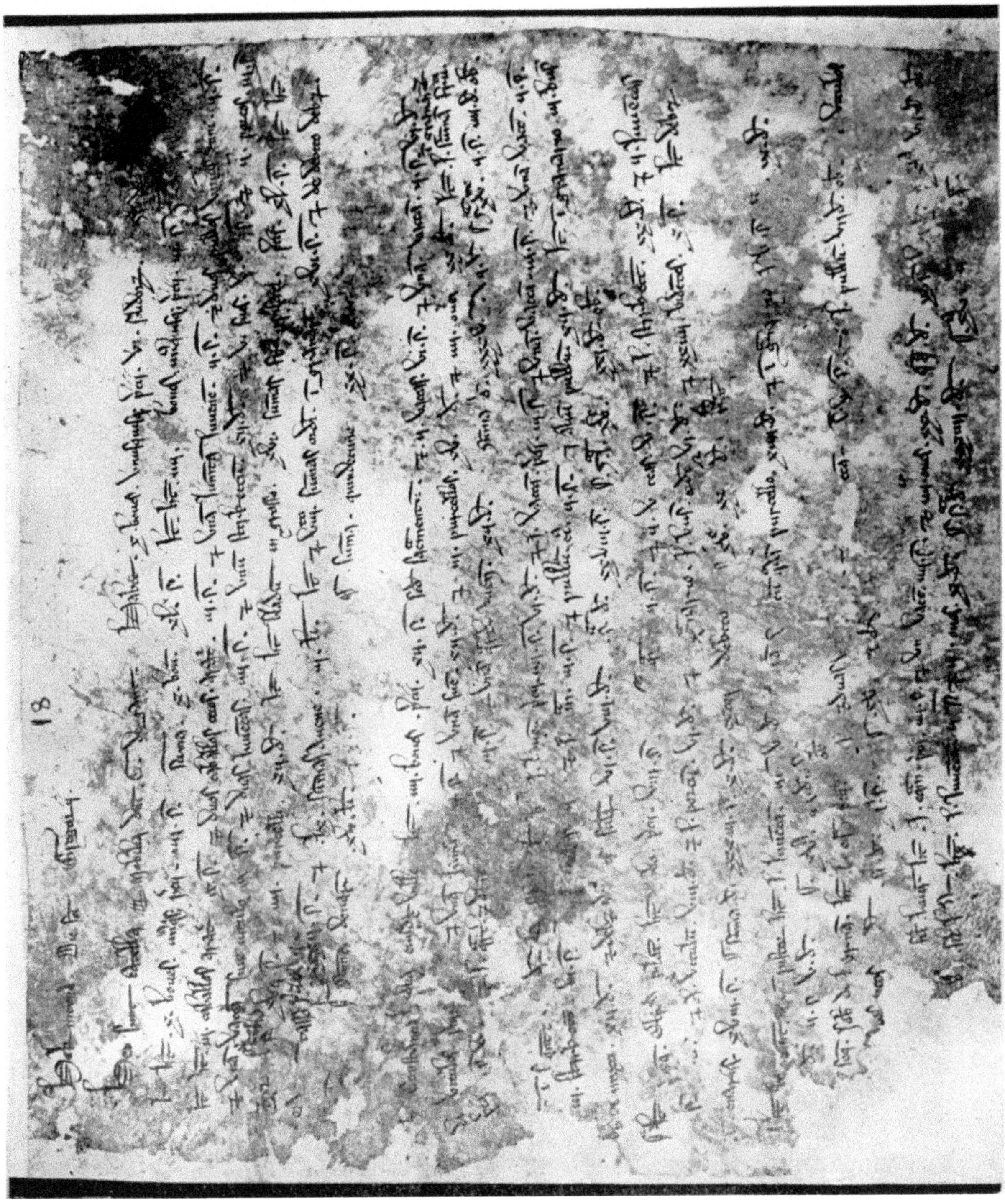

PLATES XII AND XIII

Plates XII and XIII may be treated together, the noticeable features appearing most strongly in XIII.

Attention might be called to numerous 'advanced' features such as the doubled head of long *s* and the completely artificial *w* (entirely unlike a double *v*). But these are little more than repetitions of points noticed in Plate XI. There is, however, in these two plates, and particularly the second, one matter of outstanding interest sufficient by itself to distinguish them from all the others. That is the use everywhere of the wedge-shaped mark for all diagonal and horizontal strokes, particularly the final part of *d* and the ordinary superior abbreviation mark. This, of course, gives us what might be the hand of an up to date scribe in almost any year after the earliest part of Henry III's reign.

A particularly useful comparison, or contrast, may be made between this Plate and Plates III and VII.

Plate XIII

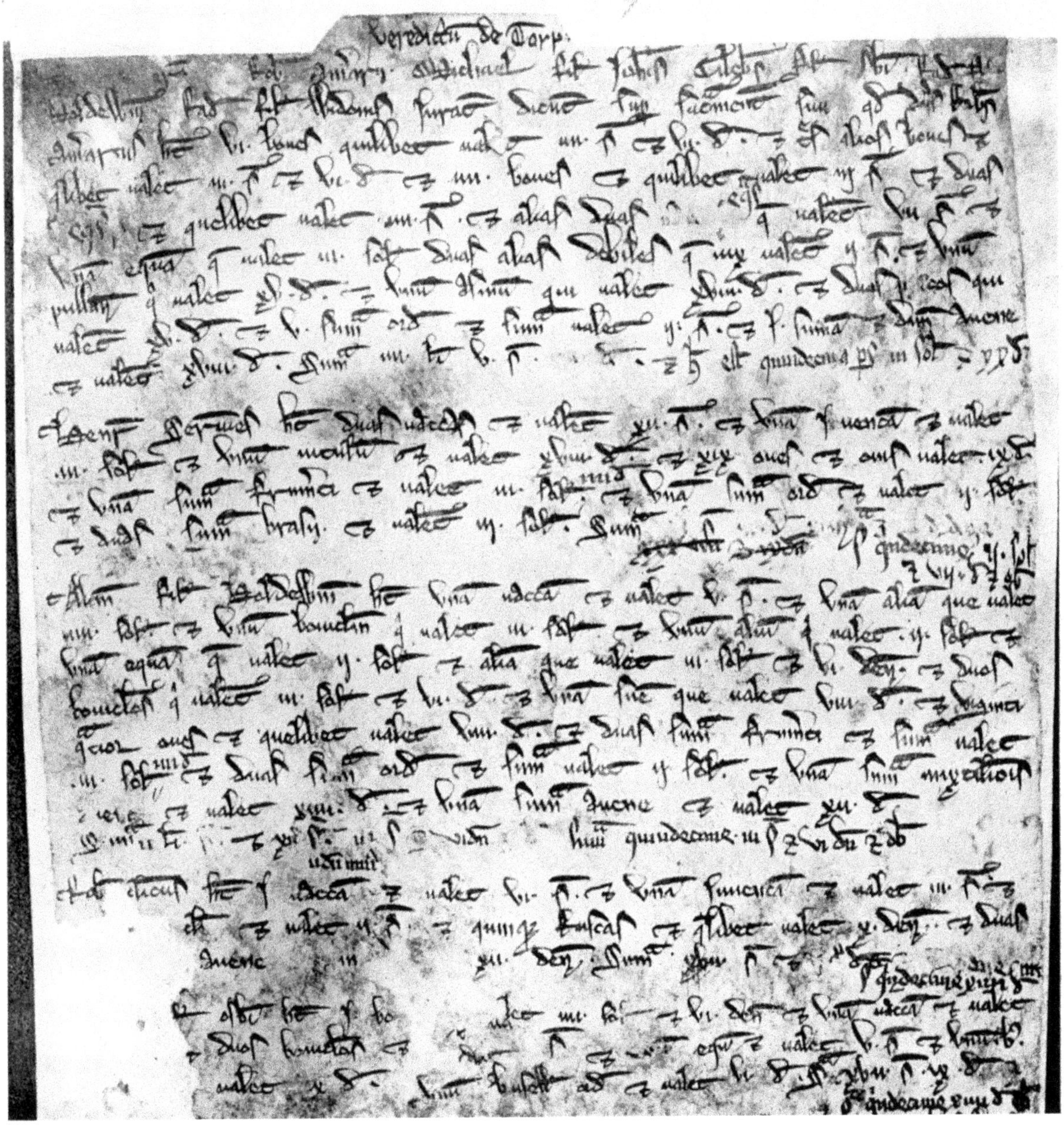

I hope, even if the similarities which I have traced in one or two cases to definite Documents elsewhere may not be followed, it will at least be agreed that this interesting collection exhibits a large number of handwritings very markedly differentiated. Their value for the purposes of illustration to which I referred is this:

(1) They represent writings made by men in quite a humble position —tax collectors or their agents; there must have been hosts of men like these spread over the Kingdom.

(2) What is more important, these documents *are all of one date*—1225; they all relate to the same small piece of business; they actually form separate membranes of a single roll[1]; and they come all from one small part of Lincolnshire not more than a few miles square. I know of no other single document so happily exemplifying a large number of early handwritings which are contemporary and yet quite distinct; except perhaps the *Rouleau Mortuaire du B. Vital*, published in facsimile by Delisle.

CONCLUSION

I do not wish for a moment to maintain the absurd proposition that the reading of medieval Documents is best acquired purely by rule of thumb; that there are no rules of abbreviation, no facts with regard to the formation of a given letter in (let us say) the 12th and again the 15th centuries which an experienced teacher may profitably communicate to an inexperienced student, to the great saving of the latter's time. My aim is merely to suggest that when we say Palaeography we do not mean the mere teaching of a student to read medieval documents—that we must be prepared to abide by the real meaning of the word: and to shew that the importance of Palaeographical Science is at present overrated, while that of the History of Administration is dangerously undervalued, in relation to the solution of normal difficulties in the reading of Court Hand and to the training of students for the purposes of Historical research. The result of this is, of course, that a great deal of time is given unnecessarily to Palaeography, while (an even more serious matter)

[1] Exchequer, K.R., Subsidies 242/127. The roll was found among some early Tallies transferred to the Public Record Office from the Chapel of the Pyx a few years ago. The Wiltshire returns of the same date (Subs. 242/47) may be usefully compared with it.

the student is cut off from that knowledge of Administrative History which is really vital to his work.

If I have seemed to dwell over much on what certainly should be an obvious point—that the methods of the conventional *Diplomatique* and Palaeography, invented to deal with early and sparse documents, break down when applied to the large mass of Records (so much later as these are in date and in character so insular)—it is because the trend of contemporary criticism in England leads to the supposition that this conclusion is not yet sufficiently plain to many scholars whose opinion upon the subject is a matter of great moment. Our Records are of so much value, and the proper working of them a need so pressing, that the presentment in an emphatic form of the views of the English school of Record workers seems to be of real importance. That school is one which can trace its history from Fanshawe and others in the 16th and early 17th centuries down through Madox to Maitland. It has never ceased to handle English Records, whether from the point of view of form or from that of handwriting, on the basis of an examination of administrative activities. In the matter of Palaeography its views might perhaps be summed up best in the statement that Court Hand documents can generally be read with certainty, but only in the light of their meaning; and that they can nearly always be dated with accuracy, but not by their handwriting.

www.ingramcontent.com/pod-product-compliance
Ingram Content Group UK Ltd.
Pitfield, Milton Keynes, MK11 3LW, UK
UKHW051957020325
455765UK00009B/52

9 781107 427457